IMAGES
of America

BETHEL PARK

IMAGES
of America

BETHEL PARK

Kristen R. Normile

ARCADIA
PUBLISHING

Published by Arcadia Publishing
Charleston, South Carolina

Library of Congress Control Number: 2010927622

For all general information, please contact Arcadia Publishing:
Telephone 843-853-2070
Fax 843-853-0044
E-mail sales@arcadiapublishing.com
For customer service and orders:
Toll-Free 1-888-313-2665

Visit us on the Internet at www.arcadiapublishing.com

To my entire family, especially Zachary, who gave his summer vacation to me while I wrote, and to David, who always believes in the best in me.

Contents

ACKNOWLEDGMENTS

This was truly a collaborative effort on the parts of many people who love the history of our community. Thank you to Jaime Amrhein for helping research and organize all of this information. Also, thank you to the people who contributed their time, stories, and photographs to preserve our history and helped bring this to fruition: Andy Amrhein, Richard and Patricia Kraft, Reno Virgili, Russell and Jane Smith, Gordon and Pete Edwards, Mayor Cliff Morton, Councilman Vince Gastgeb, Leonard and Mary Ann Tischler, John Walsh, Paul Henney Jr., Richard Gaetano, Vicki Flotta and the Bethel Park School District, Bill and Mary Murdoch, Sally Murdoch Schneider, Helen Masisak, George Radnick, Susan Senovich Pacacha, Mary Belback, Ron and Lynn Miller, Rick Sebak, Jim and Bonnie Puglisi, Suzanne Fagan, Denise Grantz Bastianini, Sue Miller, Mike Gregg, the Wasko family, the Yugo-Slav Club, Mark Rice and the Bethel Park Fire Department, Scott Zinsmeister and the Bethel Park Police Department, Mark O'Brien, Ray Ames, Sydney Litzenberger, Gene Schaeffer, Christine McIntosh and the Bethel Park Public Library, Jay and Nancy Wells, the Bethel Presbyterian Church, and the Bethel Park Community Foundation. I also would like to acknowledge two men I knew for only a short time, but who touched my heart with their love for Bethel Park: Dave Matragas and Jim Kling.

INTRODUCTION

On April 10, 1606, long before the original colonies were ever in the minds of the forefathers, King James I of England granted rights of settlement of the northeastern region of America to two companies: the London Company and the Plymouth Company. This agreement of property rights, known as the First Virginia Charter, allowed rights of settlement of the North American coast between 34 and 45 degrees latitude, which included what is now southwestern Pennsylvania. Thus began the migration of Europeans to America's East Coast.

In its earliest day, Bethel Park was dotted with Native American tribes, such as the Shawnee and the Delaware, who began to drift westward under pressure from the new eastern-settling Europeans. By 1787, Pennsylvania had entered the Union as the second of the original 13 colonies. It was right before this time, however, that frontiersmen started journeying westward through the Cumberland Valley region and Allegheny Mountains to begin settlements in southwestern Pennsylvania. Along with these pioneers came a Christian reverend who would ultimately lend the name Bethel to the community.

Feeling that he could bring spiritual leadership to this new area of wilderness, Rev. John McMillan traveled westward as the expansion opened up the southwestern region of Pennsylvania. In 1776, right before the onset of the Revolutionary War, McMillan started preaching to a congregation of followers in the old Stone Manse in what is now South Park. In following years, and as population grew, McMillan established two divisions of his congregation: an eastern division that he named Lebanon and a western division called Bethel. The township of Bethel took this name in 1886.

At the start of the 20th century, Bethel Township was still farmland, as was much of the land south of Pittsburgh. That began to change when industry started to grow due to advances in transportation and railroads. The Pittsburgh Terminal Coal Company built coal mines along the Montour Railroad, a short-line railroad built to move coal in rural areas of western Pennsylvania, which ran straight through Bethel Park. Mollenauer, or Mine No. 3, was built in 1902 and was the smaller of the two mining patches established by Pittsburgh Terminal Coal. It was when Pittsburgh Terminal Coal built Mine No. 8 and their "model mining housing community" in Coverdale in 1921 that workers and their families came in droves to Bethel. The convenience of the Pittsburgh Railways trolley system continued to bring workers and businesses to the area throughout the 1920s and 1930s.

By the time coal usage began to decline in the 1940s and Mollenauer and Coverdale had shut down, Bethel had grown in leaps and bounds. It had become a thriving commercial and residential suburb of Pittsburgh. In the 1940s, Bethel Township grew exponentially, and in 1949, it assumed a borough form of government and became Bethel Borough. The ease of transportation to and from the city allowed for more residential developments and commercial business to sustain a thriving suburb. By the 1970s, Bethel Borough had grown large enough to become a home rule municipality, now known as Bethel Park.

In the last decades of the 20th century, Bethel Park's population has grown to make it the largest-populated community in Allegheny County. As of the 2000 census, Bethel Park had over 33,000 residents. It touts beautiful neighborhoods and an award-winning school district with five neighborhood elementary schools, two middle schools, and, in 2012, a brand-new high school to take students, and Bethel Park, well into the 21st century.

One

THE CHURCH AND
THE FORT

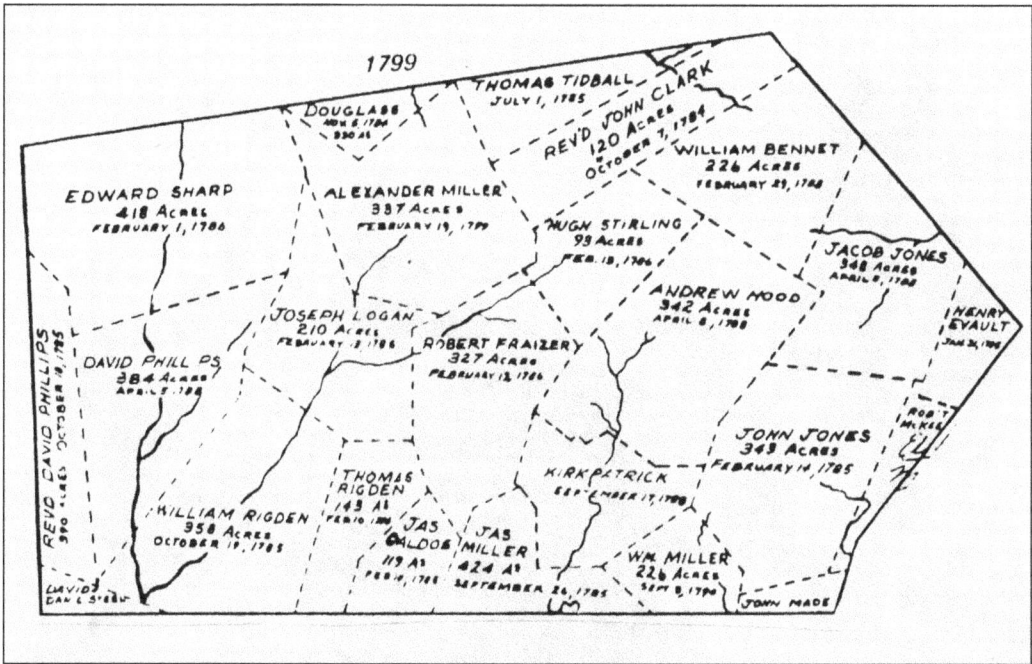

This 1799 map shows the first settlers and landowners of the area, including recognizable names like Tidball, Phillips, Logan, and Rev. John Clark. At the time, there were little more than 600 people living in the area. (Courtesy of the Smith family collection.)

The first recorded date of service at what is now Bethel Presbyterian Church was noted by Rev. John McMillan (1752–1833) in his diary on November 5, 1776: "Tuesday preached at Peter's Creek, baptized 5 children." This pioneering pastor named the western division of his Peter's Creek congregation Bethel, thus giving the community its name. (Courtesy of the Bethel Presbyterian Church collection.)

This is a rendering of the first meetinghouse of Bethel Presbyterian Church erected in 1779. It was a log structure built on an acre of land purchased from Nathaniel Couch. It is widely assumed that it was built in close proximity to Couch's Fort, which provided protection from Native American attacks. (Courtesy of the Bethel Presbyterian Church collection.)

Rev. George Marshall (1806–1872) was a Bethel landowner and the third pastor of Bethel Presbyterian Church. He and his wife, Mary Lee, were married in 1830 and lived in the parsonage built in 1838 by the Marshalls. Reverend Marshall was instrumental in starting Bethel Academy, a secondary school that was meant to prepare children for acceptance into Jefferson College (now Washington and Jefferson), where he was a trustee. (Courtesy of the Bethel Presbyterian Church collection.)

This is the original Marshall house built on land at the corner of what are now Oakhurst and Marshall Roads. The 60 acres of land that the Marshalls owned were adjacent to Bethel church. This home stayed in the Marshall family for more than 90 years until it was purchased by the Hicks family in 1928. It has been beautifully renovated and is currently owned by the Daum family. There also has been speculation about old tunnels under the home that aided slaves on the Underground Railroad. (Courtesy of the Bethel Presbyterian Church collection.)

The Pioneer Inn was a restaurant located on the old site of Couch's Fort. On July 15, 1794, disgruntled farmers of the region met here and marched on Gen. John Neville's home at Bower Hill to protest the whiskey tax of what is now known as the Whiskey Insurrection or Whiskey Rebellion. The Pioneer Inn included the original fireplace and some of the log timbers from Fort Couch in its structure before it was eventually torn down. A Lum's restaurant was built on its site, and ultimately, McDonald's bought the property and still maintains its business there today. (Courtesy of the Virgili family collection.)

The second meetinghouse of Bethel Presbyterian Church was erected in 1826. It was built on 4 acres of property purchased from Thomas and Elizabeth Tidball for $50. (A photograph of the third meetinghouse graces this book's cover.) Under the direction of Bethel Church's fourth pastor, Rev. Dr. Cornelius Wycoff (inset), the current structure shown here was erected in 1910. It had been decided that a new church would better serve the community rather than making repairs to the old meetinghouse. It was built at the cost of $30,432.32 and still stands today. (Courtesy of the Bethel Presbyterian Church collection.)

This image of the Graeser farm was fused together with the photograph below of the Hultz farm to create a landscape photograph. The photographs were taken from Bethel Church Road overlooking the two adjoining farms. At left in the distance of the above picture are Fort Couch Road and the land where South Hills Village and Village Square now stand. (Both, courtesy of the Bethel Presbyterian Church collection.)

In the late 1800s, Richard Miller Patterson and Etta Douglas Patterson originally lived at the top of Brush Run Road when they decided to move to Etta's old family farm along what is now Patterson Road. Their son J. D. was born in 1904 on the farm. He was raised there and attended (and eventually taught at) Irishtown School. (Courtesy of the Bethel Presbyterian Church collection.)

Bethel Park was, at one time, all rural farmland such as this. This is the Lutz farm on Kings School Road, where the developments of Kings School Village and Eagle Trace now stand. (Courtesy of the Virgili family collection.)

In the spring of 1792, Peter Croco purchased over 50 acres of land and built his family home, which is still located at the corner of Horning and Baptist Roads. Peter Croco was a Revolutionary War soldier and was buried on his property. Since no marker exists where he was laid to rest, a marker dedicated to Peter Croco is located in Bethel Cemetery, along with the graves of 13 other soldiers of the Revolution. Shown in front of the Croco home are, from left to right, Melinda, Beatrice, Frank, George, and Peter Croco. (Above, courtesy of the Smith family collection; below, courtesy of Richard and Patricia Kraft.)

The Irishtown Band gathers at the McMasters home in 1897. Bands like this were not uncommon at the start of the 20th century and would likely play the then-popular genre of march music: military-style music consisting of mostly horns, drums, cymbals, triangles, and bagpipes. Shown from left to right are Bill Skiles, Bart McMasters, Martin Stolze, James Elliott, Walter Eggers, Adam DeWalt, George Rothhaar, Tom Roach, George Rhodes, Martin Cummins, and John Stolze. (Courtesy of the Smith family collection.)

This pre-20th-century photograph depicts the Stolze house on Irishtown Road. The family ran Stolze Butchering. Pictured are, from left to right, (first row) Daniel, Bell, and John R. Stolze; (second row) Charles Stolze, John Dewalt, William Stolze, Martin Stolze, Adam Dewalt, Matilda Stolze (holding baby Ralph), and Katherine. (Courtesy of the Smith family collection.)

This is a photograph of the Matthews farm in the 1930s. The farmhouse stood on South Park Road, near the intersection of Logan Road, until it was torn down in 2009. (Courtesy of the Smith family collection.)

The Murdoch family home, built in the 1940s at the top of Kings School Road, has been lovingly renovated and still stands there today. (Courtesy of William Murdoch.)

Lytle Road was named for the early Lytle family settlers. The Lytle homestead still stands near the corner of Lytle Road and Applegate Avenue. (Courtesy of the Smith family collection.)

The Heile house, built by real estate broker James Heile in 1906, still stands at the corner of Highland and West Library Avenues. It was one of the first homes built in what was originally called Summit Park, the first housing development in Bethel. (Courtesy of Denise and Keith Bastianini.)

An old car is seen driving up Route 88 from the intersection of South Park Road, Baptist Road, and Corrigan Drive past land just beginning to be developed into commercial and residential property. (Courtesy of the Studt family collection.)

This view is taken from the Studt farm overlooking a bumper crop of cabbage toward Route 88 and South Park Road. At the top of South Park Road is the silhouette of the schoolhouse and Bethel Senior High School. (Courtesy of the Studt family collection.)

20

Two

LIFE IN A MINING TOWN

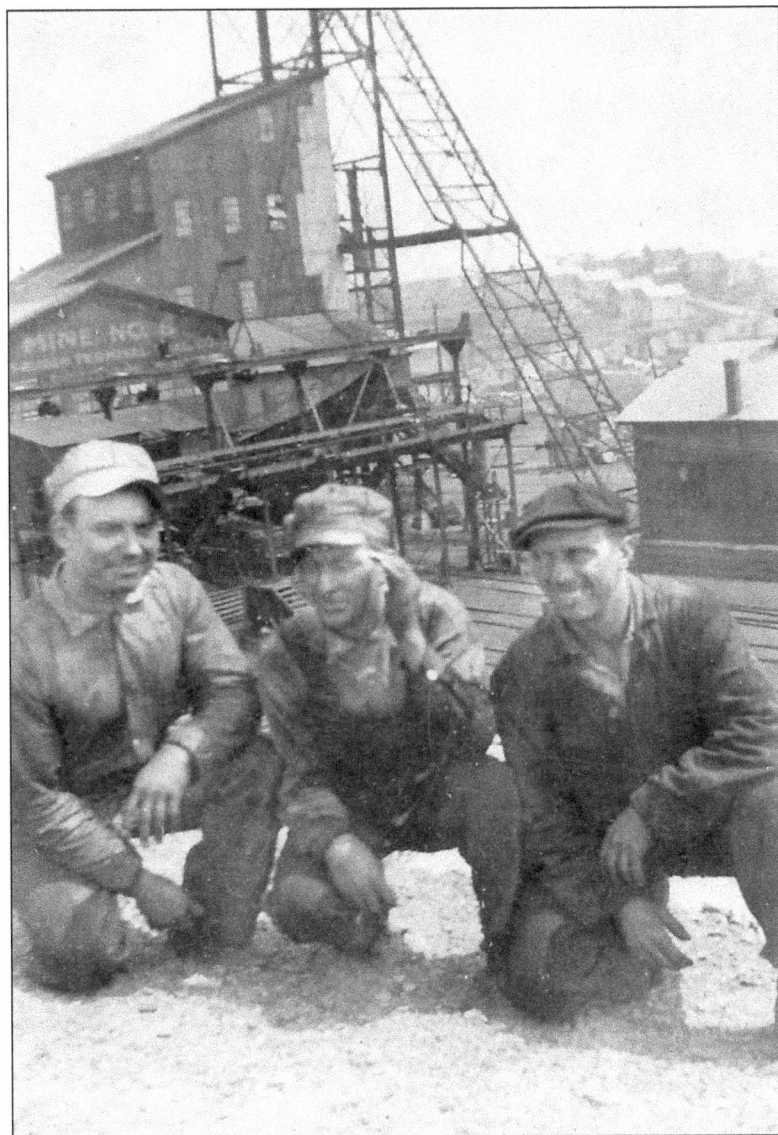

The dirt and soot carried on the clothing and faces of men tell the story of life underground. Joe Miller (far right) and two unidentified miners are kneeling outside of the Pittsburgh Terminal Coal Company Mine No. 8 in front of the Coverdale tipple. (Courtesy of Ronald Miller.)

Mollenauer was the first mining development built in Bethel by the Pittsburgh Terminal Coal Company in 1902. It produced coal until 1939. (Courtesy of the Wasko family collection.)

The Mollenauer "patch" houses filled the landscape from Washington Junction up toward Bethel Church Road and Hillcrest. (Courtesy of the Wasko family collection.)

Main Street, the entrance to the homes of Coverdale, was beginning to take shape in the early 1920s. At the time when Coverdale was developed, it was considered a model mining community. (Courtesy of the Radnick/Gerdich family collection.)

This was the bathhouse for the miners at Coverdale. After working all day, miners would come here to clean up before going home. (Courtesy of the Radnick/Gerdich family collection.)

These children gathered in the street of Coverdale, more than likely to go to school or the mission Sunday school. The streets were dirt and rock, and there was very little green left after the company cleared the land for development. (Both, courtesy of the Bethel Presbyterian Church collection.)

Steve Radnick was a miner in Coverdale and other mines after Mine No. 8 closed in 1947. His brother George wrote "An Ode to a Miner," which was dedicated to him. It is engraved on Steve's headstone in Bethel Cemetery. (Courtesy of the Radnick/Gerdich family collection.)

Pittsburgh Terminal Coal Company built over 200 houses in the Coverdale patch, one of the largest in the region. They were two-story, four-room houses cramped closely together. There was only one outhouse for every two houses. They had only a coal stove for heat in the winter and no basements. (Courtesy of the Bethel Presbyterian Church collection.)

This is a view looking toward the slate dump and over the company houses of Coverdale. It was said to have a constant glow from the red-hot slate dumped from the coal mine. It also created a constant odor, which hung in the air over the patch. The lower part of Coverdale was called "Mexico" or "Little Mexico" due to the large population of ethnic workers and their families. (Courtesy of the Puglisi family collection.)

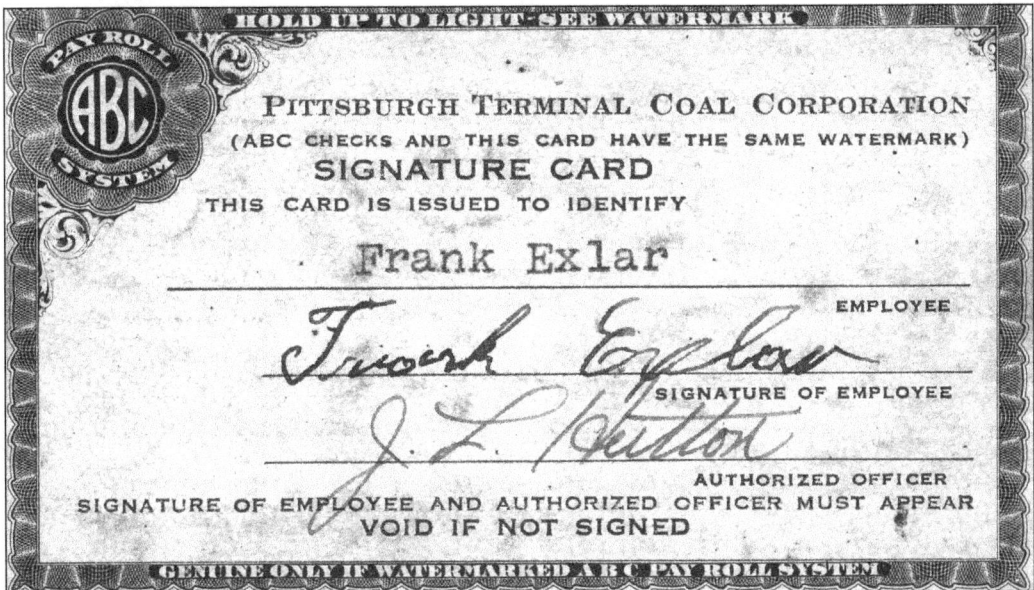

This was a standard identification card for Pittsburgh Terminal Coal employees. They used it for payroll and other work-related identification. Frank Exler was a miner at Mine No. 8. (It also was not uncommon for names to be misspelled, as was Exler's.) (Courtesy of Bob Exler.)

The Coverdale company store, Mutual Supply Company No. 8, originally started in the basement of an old house on East McKeesport Washington Boulevard, better known now as South Park Road. In 1930, it opened this store in Coverdale on Main Street. It was operated by the McChesney family. (Both, courtesy of George Radnick.)

These Coverdale and Mollenauer tokens are actually called scrip. Miners were often paid in scrip that was only good in the local mine's company store, where all their provisions, tools, food, and clothes were purchased. The stamped M and C made them easily identifiable to the store's employees. (Both, courtesy of Richard Gaetano.)

These houses on Church Road were called black shanties because they had black tar paper for siding. They were a common sight during the mining era in Bethel Park. (Courtesy of Radnick/Gerdich family collection.)

On an early spring Friday, March 11, 1927, Paul Jaworski and his notorious Flathead Gang waited in the brush on what is now Brightwood Road, close to the intersection of Route 88, for the armored truck that carried the Coverdale miners' weekly payroll. With the push of a plunger, the explosives that the gang had buried just beneath the surface blew a huge hole in the road and sent the armored car into the air, causing it to land upside down. Its convoy car was driven into the crater left by the blast, and in the melee, the thieves made off with $104,000. Fortunately, no one was killed, and 48 hours later, Jaworski was captured. It is acknowledged as the first documented armored-car robbery in the United States. (Courtesy of private collection.)

In the 1930s and 1940s, most coal mining towns had soccer teams. Coverdale was no exception. The Coverdale team was formed in 1938–1939 and played in the Panhandle League. They won the championship in 1940. Pictured below are, from left to right, (first row) Bingo Beadaling, Jim McCracken, Joe Mercer, Stan Buchek, Walt Buchek, Tom Brown, and Noris Mercer; (second row) Dan Webb, Charlie Kost, Charlie Phillips, Joe O'Farrell, Chester Sackinsky, Jap Toci, Bill Matthews, and John Miskunas. (Above, courtesy of the Yugo-Slav Club; below, courtesy of the Virgili family collection.)

This was not an uncommon scene in Coverdale during the 1930s. Tereza Radnick Gerdich lived on Idaho Street off of Church Road. She is doing the laundry in her backyard under an apple tree. (Courtesy of Susan Senovich Pacacha.)

Many Yugoslavic immigrants migrated to Bethel Park and the Pittsburgh area. The Radnick brothers—from left to right, Matthew, Anthony, Michael, and Joseph—came to this area at the beginning of the 20th century from Pisarovina, Yugoslavia. Anthony Radnick was killed when he was hit in the head with a bottle during a union strike in Coverdale. (Courtesy of Susan Senovich Pacacha.)

Rose Puglisi stands outside her home in Coverdale on Cherry Street. She raised 12 children in her small company home. It was not uncommon for families to have as many as 8, 10, or even 12 children living in these tiny four-room houses. (Courtesy of the Puglisi family collection.)

Alfia "Rose" Puglisi came to America from Sicily, Italy, in 1912 with her husband, Salvatore, who began working in the Coverdale mine. She had to renew her U.S. Alien Registration Card on a yearly basis. (Courtesy of the Puglisi family collection.)

Alien Registration No. 301365

Name Alfia Rose Puglisi
(First name) (Middle name) (Last name)

RIGHT INDEX FINGERPRINT

(Signature of holder) Alfia Puglisi
16—26150-1

Birth date Dec 15 1901
(Month) (Day) (Year)

Born in or near Passo Chero Catano Italy
(City) (Province) (Country)

Citizen or subject of State of Italy
(Country)

Length of residence in United States 30 yrs., 0 mos.

Address of residence 580 Cherry St
(Street address or rural route)

Coverdale Alleg Pa.
(City) (County) (State)

Height 5 ft., 1 in.

Weight 143 lb.

Color of hair Black

Distinctive marks Mole Right side Nose

Edward W Welch
(Signature of Identification Official)

Application filed in Alien Registration Division. Copy filed with Federal Bureau of Investigation office at

PITTSBURGH, PA.
16—26150-1

PITTSBURGH FEB 20 1942 REGISTERED

33

The Coverdale Mission was built in 1929 for the purpose of religious instruction for the area's children. The mission served the area until it closed in 1962. (Courtesy of the Bethel Presbyterian Church collection.)

Teacher Karla Strobl is pictured with one of her classes outside the mission. Strobl was crucial in creating a stable, safe, and educational environment for the children of Bethel Park at the Coverdale Mission. (Courtesy of the Bethel Presbyterian Church collection.)

Karla Strobl came to America with her sister Martha in 1921 knowing only about a dozen words of English. They attended the Presbyterian Missionary Training School in Coraopolis and graduated in 1925. She found her way to Bethel and was hired as a teacher, missionary, and social worker in Coverdale. She spent her life inspiring the children of Coverdale and other Bethel neighborhoods. (Courtesy of the Bethel Presbyterian Church collection.)

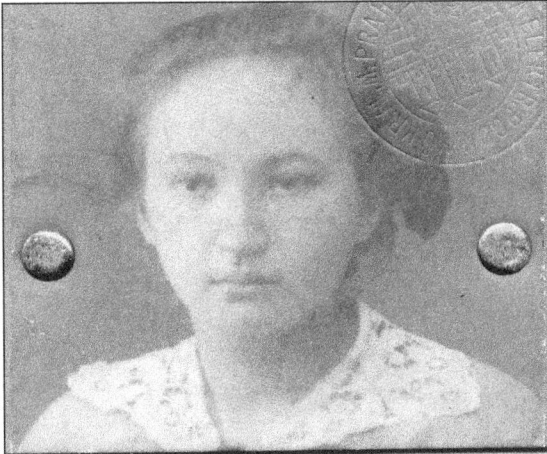

Elektrické dráhy král. hlav. města Prahy.

Rok 1916

Lístek předplatní čís. 2570

Podpis
majitelův: *Karla Stroblová*

Byt: *Praha III. Dobrovského 554*

Čitelný podpis (jméno, příjmení a byt) vyplní majitel inkoustem. Lístek bez podpisu nebo bez cenné známky nebo s cennou známkou poškozenou je neplatný.

This sight today would have parents in big trouble; however, back in the 1930s and 1940s, it was typical for trucks to gather neighborhood children and bring them to and from school. Although Karla Strobl is sitting in the driver's seat, it is more than likely she sat there just for the picture. (Courtesy of the Bethel Presbyterian Church collection.)

This photograph was taken outside of the schoolhouse where Coverdale Mission girls were happily taking a hayride. The mission offered many activities for children to do in addition to educational services. (Courtesy of the Bethel Presbyterian Church collection.)

Again, traveling by truck was the way to transport children before buses. These children were on their way to the Pittsburgh Zoo for a field trip. (Courtesy of the Bethel Presbyterian Church collection.)

Coverdale children stand outside with their prayer books or schoolbooks. (Courtesy of the Bethel Presbyterian Church collection.)

Women stand outside the Coverdale Mission holding their babies. A clinic was created in the basement of the mission and was equipped solely on the generosity of the people of Coverdale and the surrounding areas. (Courtesy of the Bethel Presbyterian Church collection.)

A bride and groom, with their flower girl, marry outside in Coverdale in the 1930s. (Courtesy of the Bethel Presbyterian Church collection.)

From left to right, Rose, Salvatore, and Jim Puglisi pose outside their house in Coverdale on a friend's car. (Courtesy of the Puglisi family collection.)

Guerrino Virgili built and ran Coverdale Bowling Lanes, a popular spot for friendly recreation across from the entrance to Main Street in Coverdale. (Courtesy of the Gene P. Schaeffer collection.)

This shows the inside of Coverdale Bowling Lanes. The building is still there today, and the lanes are still underneath the floors that have been laid down on top of them. (Courtesy of the Virgili family collection.)

Coal is delivered to the homes in Mollenauer. (Courtesy of the Virgili family collection.)

This photograph shows the slope of Hickory Street in Coverdale and the immensity of the slate dump at the end of the road in the 1940s. (Courtesy of the Virgili family collection.)

Coverdale has paid homage to the hardworking miners of Bethel Park by creating memorials in their honor. The honor roll above stood on Main Street, between Cedar and Maple Streets, to honor the United Mine Workers at Coverdale. It was eventually taken down, and the new Miner's Memorial (right) was created in Coverdale at Miner's Park, spearheaded by longtime Bethel businessman Paul Henney. (Above, courtesy of the Yugo-Slav Club; right, courtesy of Paul Henney Jr.)

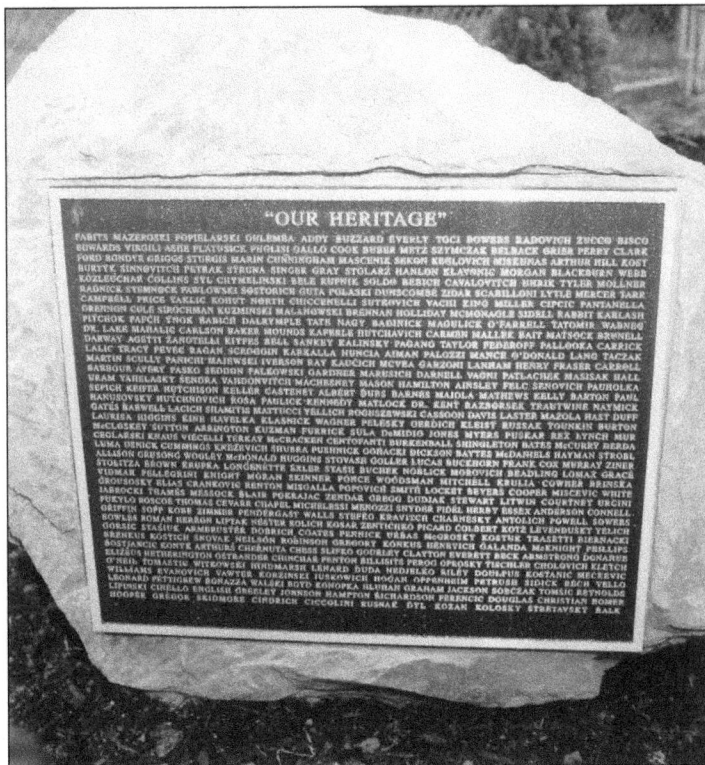

"OUR HERITAGE"

The Yugo-Slav Club is one of the oldest clubs in Bethel Park and is synonymous with coal mining history in the community. This was the original club when it was established in 1927. The club is now located at the corner of Pennsylvania Avenue and Bertha Street. (Courtesy of the Yugo-Slav Club.)

This rugged, old coal miner, carved by Kypp Pettiford from a silver maple, has stood outside the Yugo-Slav Club for years as a symbol and reminder of the proud, diligent men who worked tirelessly in the mines of Coverdale and Mollenauer. (Author's collection.)

Three

BUSINESS BEYOND COAL

As the coal industry grew in the early half of the 20th century, so did businesses around Bethel Park. Slater's was initially started in 1921 by H. A. Slater as a seed and feed supply store for local farmers in Bethel. In 1942, C. E. Walther and John McCabe purchased the business and expanded it into a gardening and home supply store. It remained open until the beginning of the 21st century and is now the Port Authority parking lot at Lytle. (Courtesy of the Virgili family collection.)

P. S. Edwards (left) was instrumental in the development of housing in Bethel during the 1920s. In fact, he had the Montour Railroad install a siding for lumber and building supplies necessary to his business. In 1926, he founded Brookside Lumber and Supply Company, a full-service contractor and home center company that he named for the newest housing plan in Bethel, where he was building. His business grew and expanded through the suburban housing boom in Bethel and South Hills. His sons Pete and Frank also ran the family business, and today it is still operated by the Edwards family and one of the area's finest and well-respected contractor suppliers and home centers. (Both, courtesy of the Edwards family collection.)

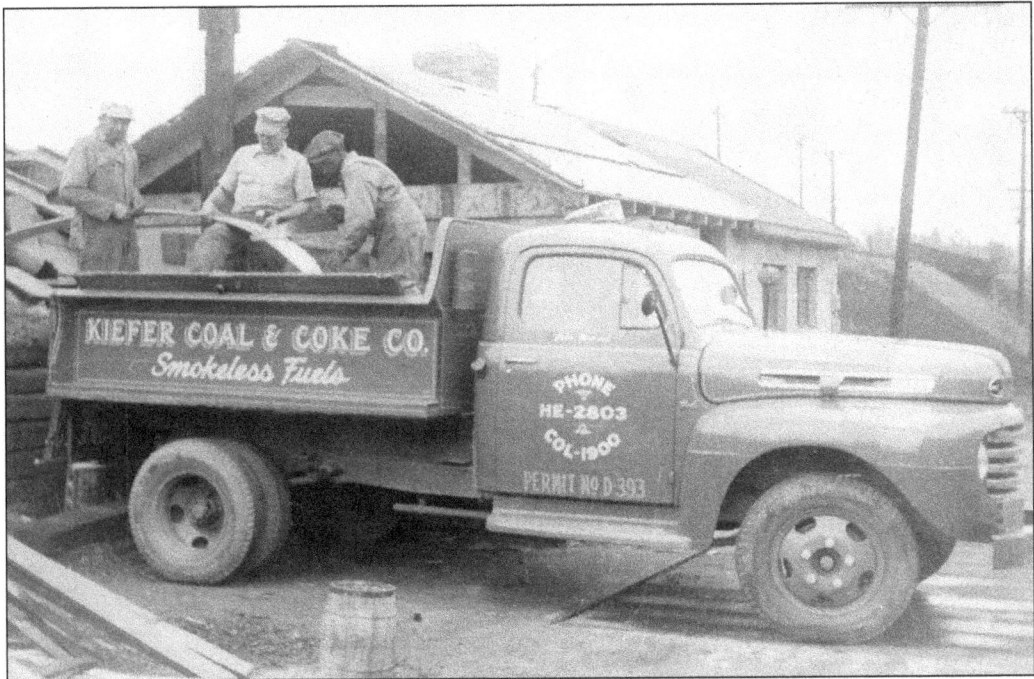

In 1930, Charles A. and Charles C. Kiefer started Kiefer Coal and Coke Company on the South Side at the corner of Becks Run Road and East Carson Street. In 1933, they purchased land and rented side track along the Montour Railroad for coal stockpiling and storage in Bethel Park. Charles C. Sr. put his 17-year-old son, Charles A. Jr. (below), in charge of this location. In 1953, when coal usage started dropping, they expanded the business to include gravel, stone, and concrete, and they renamed the business Kiefer Coal and Supply Company. Jane Kiefer Smith and her husband, Russell, took over the business in 1993, when Charles Jr. passed away at the age of 77. Their sons Russell and Daniel also work there today and are aiming to become fourth-generation owners. (Both, courtesy of the Smith family collection.)

In 1928, with just one cow, W. G. Hartman started Hartman Dairy at his farm on Bethel Church Road. His business grew rapidly, and by 1949, Hartman Dairy had acquired eight modern trucks and delivered close to 1,200 gallons of milk, buttermilk, chocolate milk, cream, and other dairy products daily. (Both, courtesy of the Virgili family collection.)

The Tischler name is one that is synonymous with the growth and development of Bethel Park. Alexander Morris "A. M." Tischler was a prominent landowner in Bethel Park. In fact, Bertha Street was named for his wife, Bertha Tischler. The photograph at right shows A. M. Tischler; his wife Bertha; his oldest son, Melvin; and his stepdaughter, Sadie. In 1921, Tischler bought property on Brightwood Road, and in 1935, they opened Tischler's Sweet Shop. They expanded their business into the two apartments above the store in 1940. A. M. Tischler was an entrepreneur and started many endeavors. One of the local favorites with the young, and young at heart, (besides the Sweet Shop) was Tischler's Grove, where he had picnic groves and a dance pavilion. He also helped organize the Bethel Fire Department and started managing real estate. (Both, courtesy of Leonard and Mary Ann Tischler.)

Tischler's younger son, Leonard, was born in 1919, and when he was old enough, he worked in the Sweet Shop seven days a week while also going to school. He graduated from Bethel High School in 1937. In 1951, he married his sweetheart, Mary Ann. She owned and operated the hair salon Tish-Tish along the side of their expanding shopping center. Leonard and his brother Sam started working together as builders and developers in the 1950s. By 1973, they worked in real estate and property management and started Tischler Brothers. Today Mary Ann and Leonard still work side by side at Tischler Brothers in the same building where his father began his Sweet Shop 75 years ago. (Courtesy of Leonard and Mary Ann Tischler.)

The Virgili family has been successful business owners and operators in Bethel Park since the 1920s. Guerrino Virgili owned several different establishments on South Park Road, including two taverns, a bowling alley, and still today, a beer distributing company that was started after Prohibition to help supply the taverns with more beverages. His son Reno Virgili and Reno's daughters still run the daily business as well as managing the family's real estate holdings. Reno Virgili grew up in Bethel Park and has been a prominent face in the community as mayor and fire chief. (Courtesy of the Virgili family collection.)

Castanet Dodge was one of the first Dodge dealers in the area. The Castanet family is shown here outside the dealership's location on South Park Road, the current site of Kozel's. (Courtesy of the Virgili family collection.)

Bethel Park afforded many opportunities for business growth and development as it expanded in the mid-1900s. The Knaus family has owned and operated many businesses in Bethel Park since that time. Along with other endeavors, Bill Knaus owned and operated a pharmacy and started the Colonial Taxi Company. His son David still owns and operates Keystone Coach Works along Route 88 in Bethel Park. (Courtesy of the Virgili family collection.)

The Miller family has owned and operated their Bethel Park business since 1937. The Miller brothers—from left to right, Steve, Billy, John, Rudy, and Joe—started their own service station along Brightwood Road. Joe's son Ron (little boy in front), a talented local drummer, was close to his father and uncles and ultimately took over the business, running it today with his wife, Lynn. (Both, courtesy of Ronald Miller.)

Miller Brothers became Miller Motor Company in the 1950s, and cars were even sold from the showroom floor. (Courtesy of Ronald Miller.)

Galliford's Crispette Company was a confectionery store that sold candy, nuts, popcorn, and other tasty treats on Bethel Church Road. It was started by Howard and Catherine Galliford (shown above) in 1929. Today the building still stands, better known as the American Legion building. (Courtesy of the Smith family collection.)

Morris "Moe" Walsh grew up on Braun Road in Bethel Park on his aunt and uncle's farm. In 1956, after he served in the navy, he came back to Bethel and married Anna Stockhausen, also a Bethel High School graduate. Walsh had started working as a teenager at Dudt's Bakery in Mount Lebanon, and in 1955, at the age of 27, he partnered with a friend and purchased the old Sugar and Spice shop on South Park Road and opened Bethel Bakery. Only 10 weeks after the opening of Bethel Bakery, Walsh's partner pulled out, and he became the sole owner. Moe and Anna are pictured below in the bakery. The first ovens (left) and counters (below, opposite page) at the Sugar and Spice location of Bethel Bakery are also shown. (Both, courtesy of the Walsh family collection.)

In only a few years, Bethel Bakery expanded its business and moved to its current location on Brightwood Road in what is now Tischler Town Centre. The business was passed on to Moe and Anna's son, John, and his wife, Chris, in 1991. Bethel Bakery's French buttercream icing has made their cakes famous, not only in Bethel Park, but all around the southwestern Pennsylvania area. (Both, courtesy of the Walsh family collection.)

The Belback family has owned the land at the corner of Route 88 and Baptist Road for over 75 years. In the late 1940s, Ray and Mary Belback operated a bike stand and hot dog shop at the entrance to South Park Road. The cyclist on top of the building was an actual moving figure made with 2-foot-by-4-foot boards and a small motor to catch the attention of people passing by. Below is a photograph of Ray and Mary on their bicycle built for two. (Both, courtesy of the Ray Belback family collection.)

The Shetland Bar was also owned and operated by the Belbacks. It was located right next to the bicycle stand. The land that the bar and bike stand occupied is still owned by the Belbacks but is now home to Giant Eagle's Get Go gas station. (Courtesy of the Ray Belback family collection.)

Johnny's Restaurant was named after John Gitnik, who owned and operated it in the 1950s. It was located close to the corner of Route 88 and South Park Road, where the Old Parkside Inn was, which was owned by the Gitniks as well. (Courtesy of the Smith family collection.)

A very recognizable location and hub of Bethel Park is South Park Shops, which is owned by the Murdoch family. The Murdochs purchased the 70-acre Hutzler farm in 1948 and built South Park Shops along Route 88 and Baptist Roads, behind the Belback property, in 1959. It has undergone many transformations throughout the years, but still remains a center of high retail business traffic in Bethel Park. (Courtesy of William Murdoch.)

This McDonald's was one of the first in the area, built in the 1950s. Its huge golden arches that extended from front to back of the restaurant were instantly recognizable to motorists traveling on Route 88. It was torn down in the 1980s, and a new McDonald's took its place. (Courtesy of William Murdoch.)

56

Ruthfred Acres Shopping Center has been home to some long-standing retail businesses in Bethel Park, including Miller's Hardware, Superior Cleaners, O'Brien Pharmacy, and The Dairy Bar. (Courtesy of the Virgili family collection.)

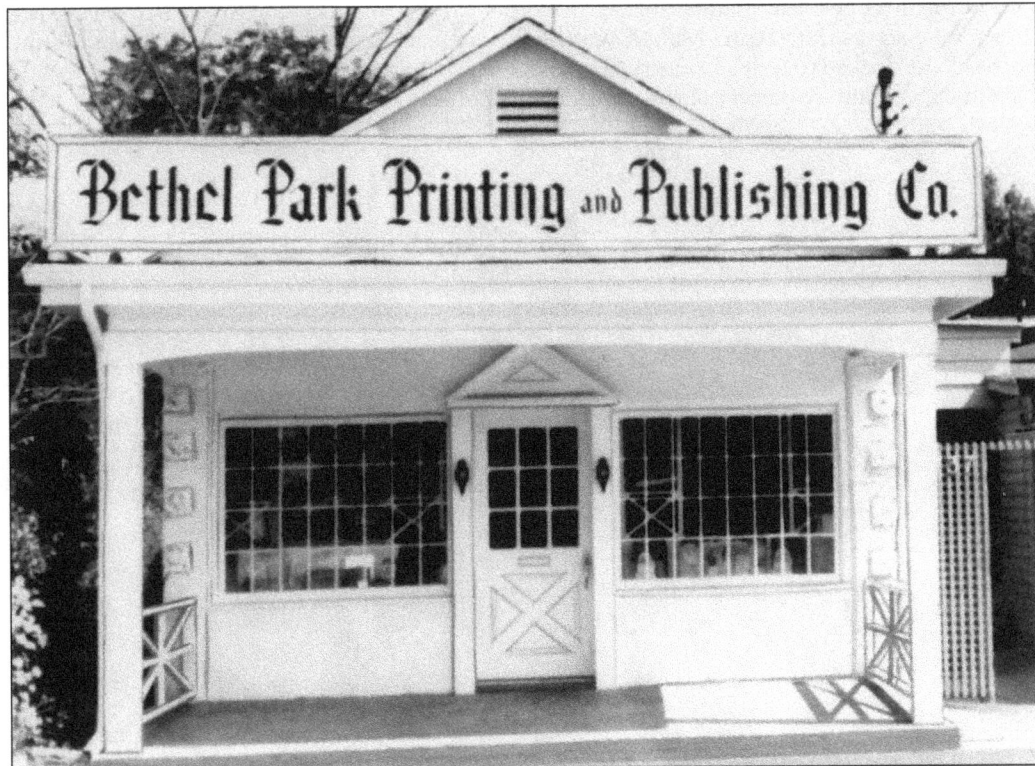

Bethel Park Printing and Publishing Company is still located on Brightwood Road, along the main business corridor. It was once Bethel Park Beverage before it became a successful printing business. (Courtesy of the Zimmer family collection.)

One of the most beloved retail businesses in Bethel Park during its suburban growth was Isaly's, shown here across from Ann's Malted Waffles. Located at the corner of Lytle Road and Route 88, residents flocked to Isaly's Country Garden for their signature skyscraper ice cream cones and chip-chopped ham. (Courtesy of the Smith family collection.)

Verscharen's was established across from South Park Shops in the 1960s. It was owned and operated by the Verscharen family and was a popular market, greenhouse, and garden supply store in Bethel Park. (Courtesy of the Smith family collection.)

The Henney family has been involved in funeral services since 1916, when the first funeral home was opened in Carnegie by H. G. Henney. In 1961, his son Paul Henney Sr. built the Bethel Park funeral home at the corner of Brightwood and Library Roads. Paul Sr.'s sons David and Paul Jr. took over the family business in 1981. In 1996, David purchased the Eugene Ocepek Funeral Home in Library, and Paul Jr. took the reins at the Bethel Park location and remains the owner of the Paul L. Henney Memorial Chapel. (Courtesy of Paul Henney Jr.)

Evey's Hardware was originally started by Edmund H. Evey Jr. on November 3, 1953, and was opened where Bethel Bakery is now. It moved into the building next to its current location two years after opening and finally to its current location at 5779 Library Road. Andy Amrhein began working there at the age of 13 in 1973. When Andy was 25, he partnered with Evey and eventually bought the company from him in 1993. He still owns and operates Evey's True Value Hardware and is there every day to open the store. (Courtesy of the Amrhein family collection.)

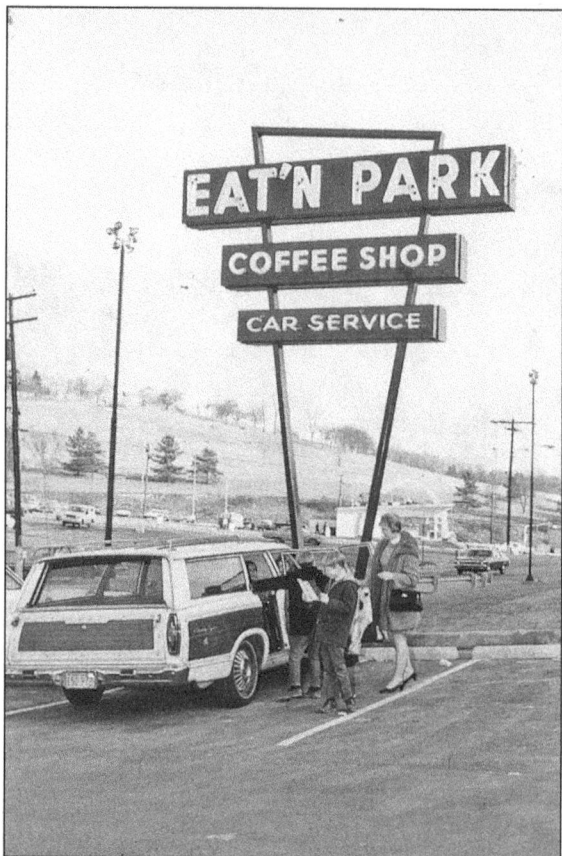

The popular restaurant Eat'n Park opened their first Bethel Park location in 1961, opposite the location where they are today on Route 88. At this location, they employed waitstaff known as carhops and offered car-side service to their customers, as well as an indoor dining area. Their "Big Boy" hamburger, seen below, was a popular choice. The Miller family, seated below, clockwise from left to right, include Ann and her children, Tom, Jim, Sue, and Karen. (Both, courtesy of the Miller family collection.)

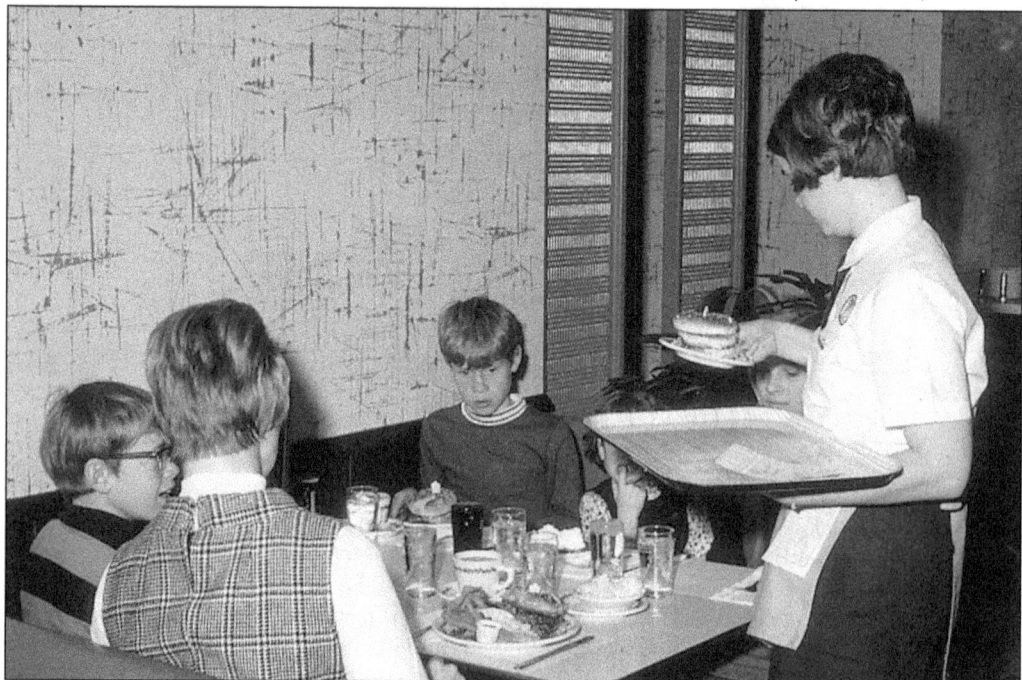

Four

TROLLEYS, TRESTLES, TUNNELS, AND TRAINS

Around the start of the 20th century, Pittsburgh Railways Interurban Division created a trolley system connecting Pittsburgh to towns south in Washington County. By the mid-1930s, Pittsburgh Railways had over 600 PCC (President's Conference Committee) cars in their fleet, just like the one shown here. In June 1953, the lines that extended into Washington County were cut back within the Allegheny County borders at Drake and Library. In 1984, Port Authority expanded this line out to South Hills Village. Today the Pittsburgh Port Authority still runs light rail vehicles (LRVs) from downtown Pittsburgh to Library and South Hills Village. (Courtesy of the Gene P. Schaeffer collection.)

PCC trolley cars cross at the old Washington Junction stop in Mollenauer. (Courtesy of the Virgili family collection.)

When the trestle over South Park Road was scheduled for removal, these "Shoofly" tracks were built alongside the line, parallel with West Library Road. (Courtesy of the Virgili family collection.)

This trestle along the Library trolley line crossed over South Park Road at the intersection of Brightwood Road. (Courtesy of the Virgili family collection.)

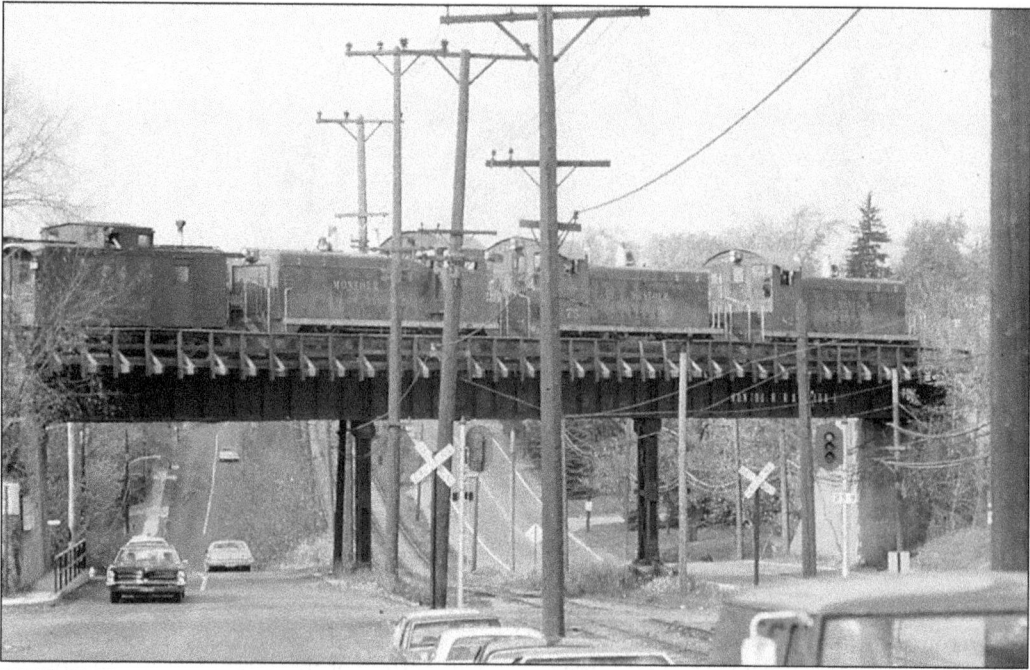

SW-9 GM locomotives Nos. 82, 75, and 80, along with red caboose No. 33, made one of their last runs along the Summit Park Bridge over Brightwood and West Library Roads on October 28, 1975. The final run along this line was December 14, 1976. (Courtesy of the Gene P. Schaeffer collection.)

On October 16, 1993, the Summit Park Bridge was removed by crane, one section at a time, over the top of the trolley lines. (Courtesy of the Gene P. Schaeffer collection.)

64

Bethel Park residents, business owners, and train buffs alike came out to see and photograph the removal of the Summit Park Bridge. (Courtesy of the Smith family collection.)

The remains of the bridge sat in a large pile at the entrance to Slater Road. (Courtesy of the Smith family collection.)

There were several tunnels along the Montour Railroad in Bethel Park. Route 88 curved through this tunnel just past Hillcrest Plaza and the Allegheny County Works Department. All the tunnels were eventually removed in the late 1970s and 1980s. (Courtesy of the Gene P. Schaeffer collection.)

Brightwood Road runs through this Montour Railroad tunnel near where the armored-car robbery took place in 1927. Across Route 88 are some familiar places from the 1970s, including Winky's, Mayfair, and Arcadian Gardens. (Courtesy of the Gene P. Schaeffer collection.)

The Norfolk and Western Railroad also ran three to four times a day on a line through Bethel Park. This grain train is running where 84 Lumber Company used to be along Baptist Road. (Courtesy of the Gene P. Schaeffer collection.)

This 1920s picture shows the Montour Railroad crossing at Horning Road. Note the handcar alongside the road with some lunch boxes sitting on top. (Courtesy of the Gene P. Schaeffer collection.)

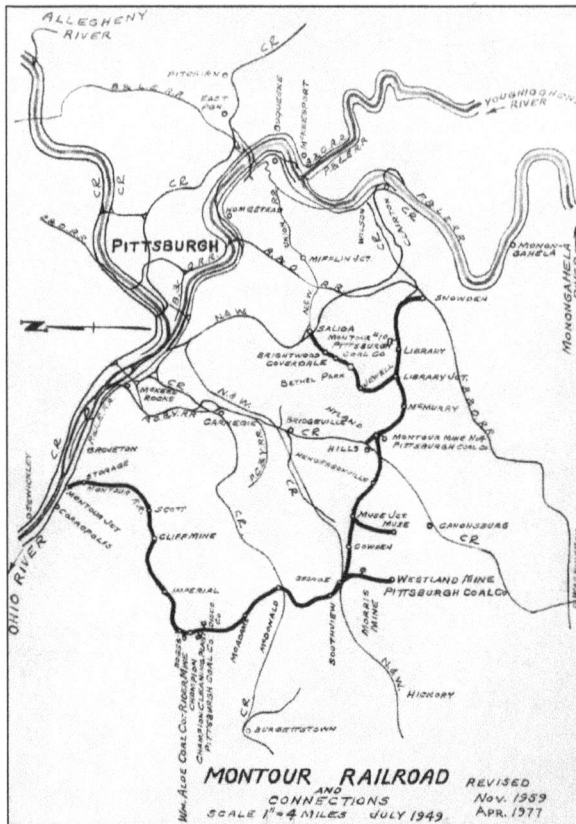

In 2000, the Pittsburgh Port Authority was letting go of four PCC trolleys, and the Bethel Park Council and Mayor Cliff Morton obtained one to commemorate the significance of PCC service and trolley transportation in Bethel Park. The trolley was hauled from the Port Authority warehouse to its present site at the schoolhouse and was dedicated in December 2000. (Courtesy of Richard and Patricia Kraft.)

This map shows the area that the Montour Railroad covered. The Montour Railroad Company was established in 1889 and ran 12 miles between Coraopolis and Imperial. In 1900, the Pittsburgh Terminal Coal Company added an additional 30 miles that ran straight through Bethel Park. The Montour Railroad is now part of national Rails to Trails project. The Montour Trail is 46 miles, and a portion runs directly through Bethel Park. (Courtesy of the Gene P. Schaeffer collection.)

Five

GOOD OLD
GOLDEN RULE DAYS

The Bethel School District was instituted in 1886 with four, one-room schoolhouses where students only attended classes six months of the year. Teachers' salaries at the time were only a little better than $200 a year. The School House Arts Building is one of the community's most recognizable landmarks. It was opened in 1905 as the Bethel Vocational School for students in first to twelfth grade. (Courtesy of the Bethel Park School District.)

King's School was one of the first four schools in Bethel; however, it was instituted much earlier. The first of three structures was built in 1836, followed by the second structure in 1856 and the final one in 1882. It was located at the corner of Kings School Road and Route 88. The structure is still part of what is now First Bethel Methodist Church. (Courtesy of the Bethel Park School District.)

Irishtown School, shown here, was built in 1886 and was another of the first four schools in Bethel. Located on Irishtown Road, where the Jehovah's Kingdom Hall is now, Irishtown School closed its doors 1937. The Croco School, built in 1860, was also one of the original four and was named for the Croco family, who lived just down the road from it. It was abandoned in 1896. The fourth school was Bethel Grade School, a structure that no longer stands. (Courtesy of the Bethel Park School District.)

The Bethel Park Historical Society now owns the old Bethel Vocational School at the corner of Park Avenue and South Park Road. The school was opened in 1905 and has been used as a vocational school, a grade school, a high school, and administrative offices. It is now open to the public as the Schoolhouse Arts Center, where many South Hills artists and craftsmen show and sell their works. (Courtesy of the Bethel Park School District.)

The bell from the old schoolhouse was removed and placed on the campus of the current high school in what is known as Bell Circle. (Both, courtesy of the Bethel Park School District.)

Bethel High School was built on Park Avenue, next to the schoolhouse, in 1927 to accommodate the growing needs of the community. It received several additions as growth in Bethel Park demanded larger facilities during the 1940s and 1950s. It was used as a junior school until it was purchased by the municipality for $1 in 1974. It was eventually razed, and the new Bethel Park Community Center and Recreation Center were built in its place. (Courtesy of the Bethel Park School District.)

Benjamin Franklin Elementary School is now one of the five remaining neighborhood elementary schools in the district. Other elementary schools have come and gone with time, including Logan and John McMillan. Ben Franklin is located on Florida Avenue, near Coverdale. It has the largest elementary school population in Bethel Park. (Courtesy of the Bethel Park School District.)

Bethel Memorial Elementary School is located on South Park Road in the Ruthfred Acres section of Bethel Park. Recently an addition was built on to the front of the school to accommodate the growing population of students in the neighborhood. (Courtesy of the Bethel Park School District.)

John McMillan Elementary School was in use up until the 1980s, when it was torn down. In its place stands the UPMC South complex and baseball field. (Courtesy of the Bethel Park School District.)

William Penn Elementary School has seen several renovations and additions after its initial opening in the 1960s, including, for a time, a satellite school created with help from the United States Steel Corporation. It is tucked back in the Boxer Heights–Irishtown Road neighborhood on Woodlet Lane. (Both, courtesy of the Bethel Park School District.)

The Pathfinder School on Donati Road is a special needs school, built in 1966, that provides educational programs and service to children with disabilities in Bethel and surrounding areas. It is run by the Allegheny Intermediate Unit and helps students between the ages of 5 and 21. (Courtesy of the Bethel Park School District.)

BETHEL   SENIOR   HIGH   SCHOOL,   BETHEL   PARK,   PA.
ALTENHOF   AND   BROWN - ARCHITECTS

The current high school was constructed as a campus-style high school in the late 1950s on what was the McCormack farm. It was initially designed for a dual purpose: Bethel Park Senior High School during the day and a community college campus in the evenings. However, it was only ever used as a high school, and it was the only campus-style high school in Pennsylvania. A new high school is currently being constructed along Church Road that will meet the needs of education going into the 21st century, and the current high school will be replaced by a state-of-the-art sports complex. (Courtesy of the Bethel Park School District.)

76

T. M. Buck (left) and R. W. Hartlieb were two early Bethel High School principals in the district. (Courtesy of the Virgili family collection.)

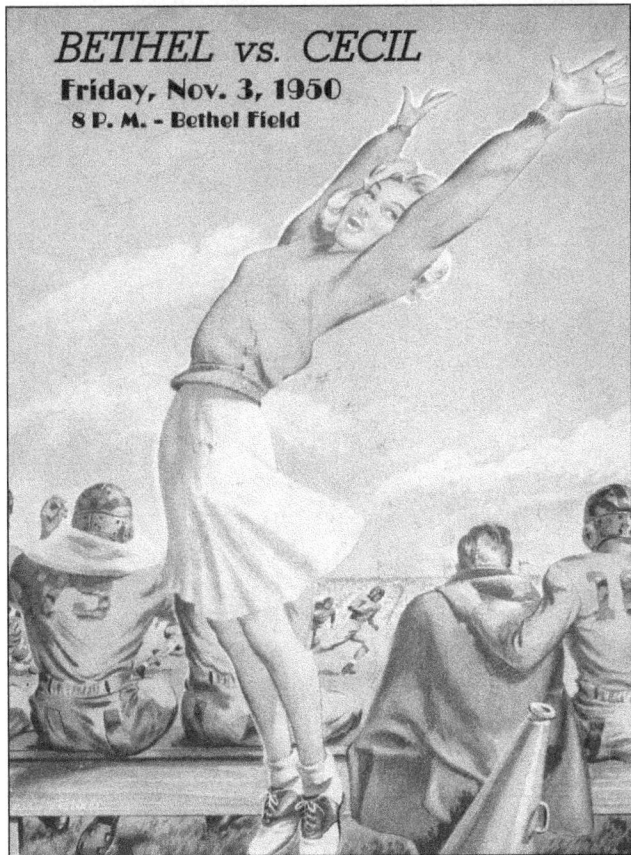

BETHEL vs. CECIL
Friday, Nov. 3, 1950
8 P. M. - Bethel Field

High school football always brings a frenzied school spirit in the fall. Bethel Park pride runs rampant during football season, and it was no exception in 1950 when Bethel played Cecil. (Courtesy of Ronald Miller.)

Bethel sports have always been widely acclaimed, and most people know Bethel Park as the Blackhawks. Initially, however, the football team was called the Bees. Above are the Bethel Bees in the 1930s. Below the Bethel Park Blackhawks' starting line takes the field in 1952. (Above, courtesy of the Virgili family collection; below, courtesy of the Puglisi family collection.)

The Bethel Park marching band started small and has grown into an award-winning marching program. Before his retirement in 2010, band director David Buetzow led the Blackhawks marching band down the streets of Pittsburgh in the Steelers Super Bowl XLIII victory parade. (Author's collection.)

The Bethettes drill team originally started as the Rangerettes in the 1940s. They soon became known as the Bethettes in their signature black outfits with white collars. Batons were eventually traded in for orange-and-white pom-poms that are highly recognizable during their precision halftime shows, festivals, and events. (Courtesy of the Bethel Park School District.)

The Bethel Park High School cheerleaders pose for the yearbook in the 1950s. (Courtesy of the Bethel Park School District.)

Bethel Park cheerleaders participate in a cheerleading competition at South Hills Village. (Courtesy of the Bethel Park School District.)

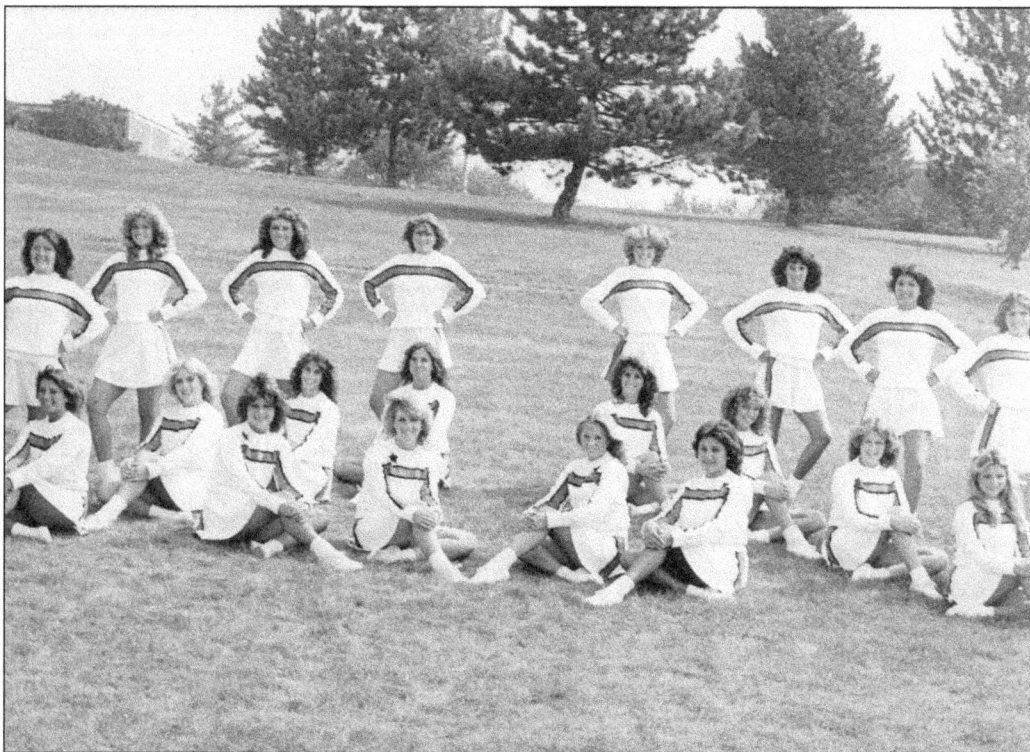

This 1981 photograph of the Bethel Park High School cheerleaders shows the difference in uniforms but the same Bethel Park pride. (Courtesy of the Bethel Park School District.)

The Bethel Park Majorettes took over the skillful talent of baton twirling and are an important part of the unique marching unit that makes up the Bethel Park High School marching band. (Courtesy of the Bethel Park School District.)

The duties of the Safety Patrol at Bethel Grade School in 1954 and 1955 were daily patrols of the school, buses, and playgrounds. (Courtesy of the Bethel Park School District.)

Students learn to type accurately in a Bethel High School typing class in the early 1960s. (Courtesy of the Bethel Park School District.)

The Hi-Y club was a group of junior and senior classmen who "aimed to create, maintain, and extend throughout the school and community, high standards of Christian life," according to the *1962 Student Handbook*. (Courtesy of the Bethel Park School District.)

Shop class, which was mainly attended by male students, has come a long way in the past 50 years. All students in fifth and sixth grade are now required to take technical education, a class that encompasses all types of new technology for education in building and engineering. (Courtesy of the Bethel Park School District.)

The Pep Club is pictured here in the early 1960s. (Courtesy of the Bethel Park School District.)

Six

FACES AND PLACES

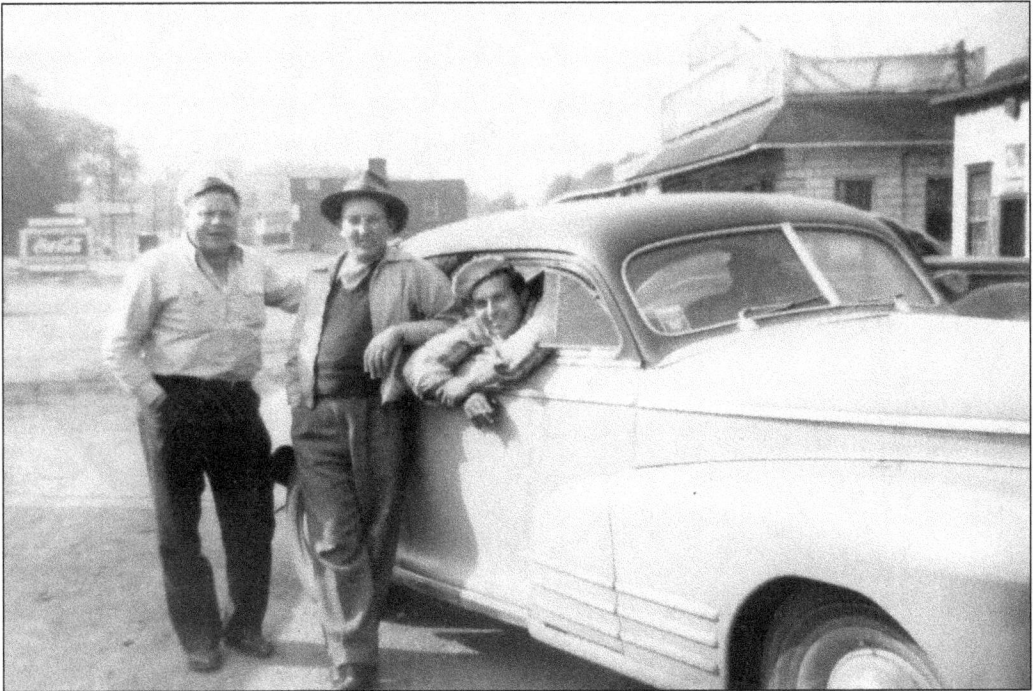

Along with great businesses and award-winning schools, it is ultimately the people and neighborhood that have made Bethel Park the strong, vibrant, successful community that it is. Steve Bittner and Rege and Wick Kiefer stopped frequently at the Shetland Bar to meet with good friends after work. (Courtesy of the Ray Belback family collection.)

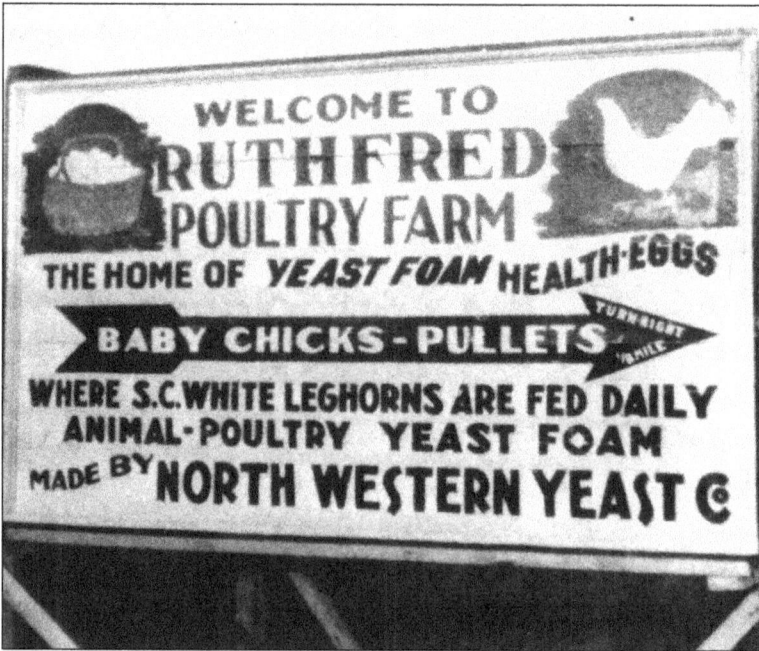

Ruth and Fred Brown owned over 70 acres of farmland along both sides of South Park Road. Initially they ran a poultry farm; however, Ruth Brown encouraged her husband to build houses on their property. The first three homes of their development were designed by Ruth, who had no formal training. Their neighborhood became known as Ruthfred Acres. (Courtesy of the Virgili family collection.)

Fred Brown wanted a lake and built one in the 1930s. He was ultimately asked to "remove" the lake for development, and he drained it not even 10 years later. (Courtesy of the Virgili family collection.)

A little girl takes a drink from the old spring house on the Brown farm in 1936. (Courtesy of the Virgili family collection.)

This is an image of Pete Edwards taken in 1933 on the Edwards property, where Brookside Lumber is located today. Toys like this were special, particularly during the Depression era. (Courtesy of the Edwards family collection.)

Helen Gerdich Masisak (left) stands with her mother, Tereza, in Coverdale, where she and her siblings grew up. (Courtesy of Helen Masisak.)

The Radnick children pose in 1924. They are, from left to right, (first row) Ann and George; (second row) Barbara and Steve. Their mother, Tereza, was asked to leave the mine housing in Coverdale after her husband died. She built a home on Idaho Avenue and married Anthony Gerdich. (Courtesy of Susan Senovich Pacacha.)

Brookside Farms was one of the earliest neighborhoods to be developed in the mid-1920s. Some houses were built in Bethel Park and some in Upper St. Clair. Brookside Farms homes were built with a lot of attention to the architectural details of the time. Katie Mumma, shown sitting by her pond, and her husband, Roy, took great care in their home gardens on Arapahoe Drive. (Both, courtesy of the Payseure family collection.)

Brookside Farms is still a highly desirable area to live due to the detailed stone-and-brick architecture and mature landscapes of the area. The Payseure home on Arapahoe Drive is shown in the mid-1900s. (Courtesy of the Payseure family collection.)

Bob Sefton (left) and Jay Wells started home development in the 1930s, after Wells's sister asked him to build a house for her on their property. They wanted to further their building plans and made a deal with Henry Offerman to build on his land and share in the profits from homes sold. They named the plan Welton Acres, a combination of Wells and Sefton's last names and built on the streets they named Old Ox, Oregon Trail, and Conestoga. (Courtesy of Dr. Jay Wells.)

As Bethel Park grew, Wells and Sefton developed more neighborhoods around Bethel, such as Meadowbrook Estates and Bethel Village. (Courtesy of Dr. Jay Wells.)

Jay Wells (left) and Gene Cassidy stand outside the Hillcrest Inn and Hillcrest Beer and Liquor along Route 88, where Hillcrest Shopping Center is today. (Courtesy of the Smith Family collection.)

The Greggs (above) were married at St. Valentine Roman Catholic Church, originally a mission of St. Anne's, in Castle Shannon. Stan and Ann Buchek (left), who owned Stan's Café on Brightwood Road, were also married in the original St. Valentine's church. (Above, courtesy of the Gregg family collection; left, courtesy of the Virgili family collection.)

The original St. Valentine's Church was formerly St. Bernard's in Mount Lebanon and was moved to the West Library Avenue site. A fire destroyed St. Valentine's on Sunday, July 19, 1942, and the new church was built in its place by 1943. A photograph of the cornerstone ceremony is shown below. (Both, courtesy of Ronald Miller.)

The Alfia Rose and Salvatore Puglisi's sons—from left to right, Mike, Carl, and Jim—had their holy communion at St. Valentine's. The church is still located at the corner of West Library Avenue and Ohio Street and has grown to meet the needs of the Catholic congregation in the area. (Courtesy of the Puglisi family collection.)

Girls from Galliford's Crispette pose in front of the sign for the new Hillcrest housing plan in the 1940s. (Courtesy of the Smith family collection.)

First Bethel United Methodist Church was formed in 1947 in the King's School building at the corner of Kings School Road and Route 88. (Courtesy of the Virgili family collection.)

The Allegheny County Fairs were held at South Park Fairgrounds adjacent to Bethel Park. Thousands of visitors would come each year, and promotional materials and gimmicks were abundant in the weeks before the event. This clown promotes the fair in front of Belback's bike stand. (Courtesy of the Ray Belback family collection.)

This image shows the early development of the Park Manor neighborhood of homes in May 1948. (Courtesy of the Virgili family collection.)

The Murdoch family moved to King's School Road in 1945. Shown sitting in the family living room are Adeline Murdoch and her children, from left to right, (first row) Frances Jean, their dog Whitey, and William Francis Jr.; (second row) Sarah Ellen and Esther Henrietta. (Courtesy of William Murdoch.)

Bonnie Risch and Jim Puglisi were dating in 1954, when Jim served in the air force. They married in 1958. (Courtesy of the Puglisi family collection.)

Fritz and Pat Verscharen take a ride through South Park. (Courtesy of the Ray Belback family collection.)

This is a view of the rolling hills of Ruthfred Acres and Patterson Road. (Courtesy of the Virgili family collection.)

Fred and Ruth Brown owned the field behind Ruthfred Lutheran Church. The Browns leased it to the church for $1 with the condition that the church agree to maintain the field and use it for children's sports. (Courtesy of the Virgili family collection.)

Recreational baseball is a favorite pastime in Bethel Park. Adults and children use the fields around the community. The Bethel Baseball Association and Bethel Church League are the two recreational children's baseball leagues of Bethel that have been around since the 1960s. Pictured above is the Danny's Tavern softball team from 1951 and below, from left to right, are Ryan Rimmel, Zachary Normile, Zachary Vinus, Tyler Hood, and Zachary Lizun of the Bethel Church League in 2006. (Above, courtesy of the Edwards family collection; below, author's collection.)

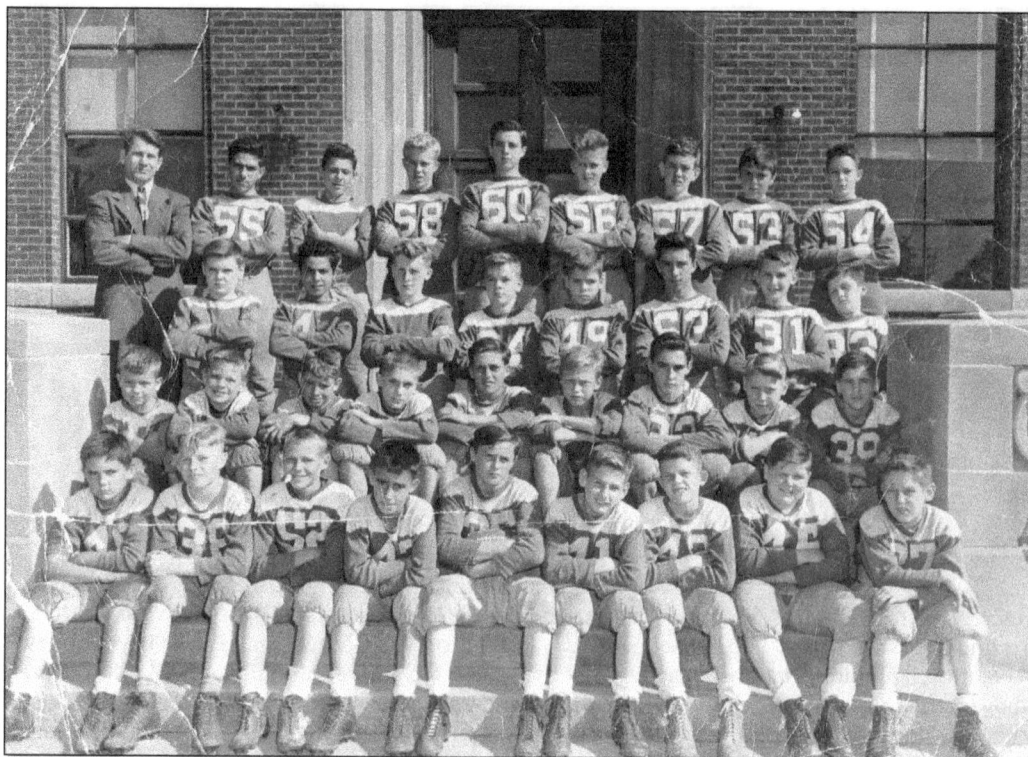

The Bethel Mites football team, in its second year in 1946, poses outside of the schoolhouse in their team uniforms. (Courtesy of the Puglisi family collection.)

Games like baseball and football have been around Bethel Park for decades, and up-and-coming sports like boys' and girls' lacrosse have added to the vast array of sports choices in Bethel Park. The Bethel Park Junior Boys Lacrosse Association was developed in the early 2000s and plays at the Park Avenue field behind the schoolhouse. Shown, from left to right, are teammates Evan Oakley, Gavin Plotz, Ben Smith, Jeremy Symsek, and Zachary Normile. (Author's collection.)

Snow is not uncommon in the Bethel Park area; however, every few decades a blizzard strikes and dumps a couple feet of snow across the area. This 1950s blizzard (right) created snow piles higher than an average man along Logan Road at Brookside Lumber. Snow in the 1960s allowed children snow days to sled down their streets. Below, from left to right, Susan, Julie, and Steven Senovich get ready to sled down Idaho and Church Streets. (Right, courtesy of the Edwards family collection; below, courtesy of Susan Senovich Pacacha.)

The storm of 2010 dumped over 22 inches of snow in one day during the first week in February. Trees were downed, power was out in many neighborhoods for days, and school was canceled for an entire week while people tried to dig out of their homes. David Normile stands outside his Boxer Heights home after spending an hour shoveling a path from the street to the door. (Both, author's collection.)

From left to right, Stevie Miller, Steve Miller Jr., Joe Miller, Eric Stutz, and Ron Miller stop to pose inside their garage. (Courtesy of Ronald Miller.)

Ron Wolfe tries to get a good spot to see President Truman's motorcade as it comes into South Park for the County Fair in the 1940s. (Courtesy of the Ray Belback family collection.)

The five-way intersection in Bethel Park was actually called "Local" at one time. This aerial view shows the intersections of Route 88, South Park Road, Baptist Road, and Corrigan Drive in the 1950s. (Courtesy of William Murdoch.)

Road construction crews get ready to pave North Lightwood Road along the trolley line. (Courtesy of the Virgili family collection.)

The Bethel Park municipal building stood where the parking lot for the current municipal building is currently located. (Courtesy of the Virgili family collection.)

The 1965 borough council meets to discuss the expanding borough. Shown, from left to right, are Mr. Schmid, Paul Hugus, Carl Watson, Ralph Bowen, Fran Shubert, Mayor Peter Page, Charles Sopp, and Reginald Bush. (Courtesy of the Virgili family collection.)

Among this group of men gathered for a softball game are Bill Chess, Dale Chess, Emil Weiner, John Augustine, Fred Taylor, Vic Hershack, Joe Versharen, Pat Kinvin, and Jim Puglisi. (Courtesy of the Puglisi family collection.)

Veteran Bethel Park police officers Scott Zinsmeister and Jim Modrak are the resource officers who assist the school district in providing a safe learning environment while developing a positive rapport with the students, teachers, and parents. Officer Zinsmeister is shown here working to ensure child safety through the Charlie Check-First identification program by Safety Kids, Inc. (Author's collection.)

106

Andy Amrhein, shown here volunteering his time and machinery to the Bethel Park Community Foundation fundraiser "Rev Up and Roll" at the South Park Fairgrounds, grew up in the Boxer Heights neighborhood of Bethel Park. He was born in his house on Kings School Road on February 22, 1960, and was raised there with his seven brothers and two sisters. The owner of Evey's True Value Hardware, he is passionate about Bethel Park and volunteers much of his time and effort to the community. He still lives in Boxer Heights with his wife, Mary Alice, and their three children—Jaime, Kathryn, and Robert. (Author's collection.)

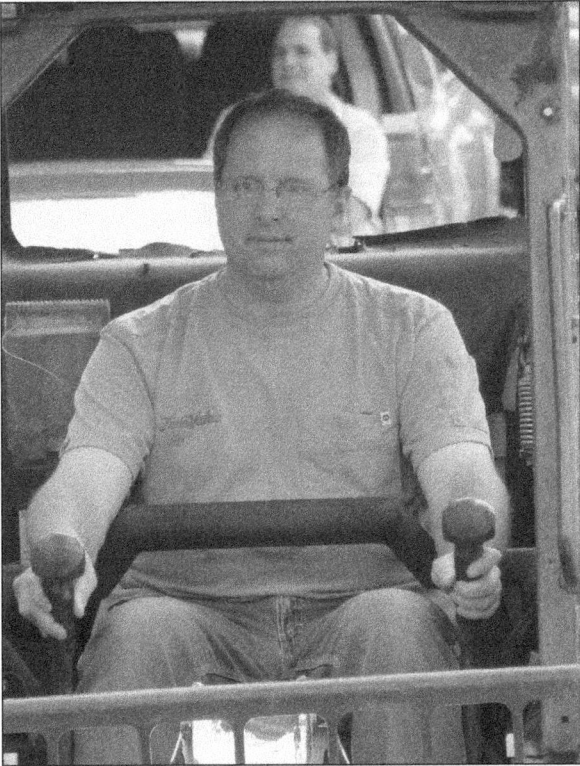

In 2000, the class of 1940 celebrated its 60th class reunion. (Courtesy of the Gregg family collection.)

This is the oldest home in the Brookside Farms plan. It has been renovated to keeps its original architecture and charm. (Author's collection.)

The McNary farm was located in what is now the Boxer Heights neighborhood of Bethel Park. The home was originally built in 1827, and the McNary family purchased it and the land in 1945. Dr. McNary was a veterinarian, and the streets in the plan were named after his four-legged patients: Dalmatian, Boxer, Great Dane, Beagle, Cocker, Airedale, Setter, Bassett, Fox Terrier, and Collie. The neighborhood subsequently became known as "the dog patch." (Author's collection.)

Mary Murdoch is holding her daughter Molly outside the groundbreaking area for the South Park Shops in 1959. (Courtesy of William Murdoch.)

A favorite entertainment for families and teenagers in the 1960s and 1970s was attending the South Park Drive-In on Route 88, next to South Park Shops. The drive-in was finally torn down, and retail businesses have since moved into its place. (Courtesy of the Gene P. Schaeffer collection.)

The Corrigan Drive pool was built in the Bethel Park portion of South Park in 1932 using the natural landscape of the area. It held 2 million gallons of water and saw thousands of visitors daily. Its beach area consisted of sand that was flown in from Spain. It eventually closed in 1977 and was turned into a roller-skating park and then the VIP Fun Center. (Courtesy of the Virgili family collection.)

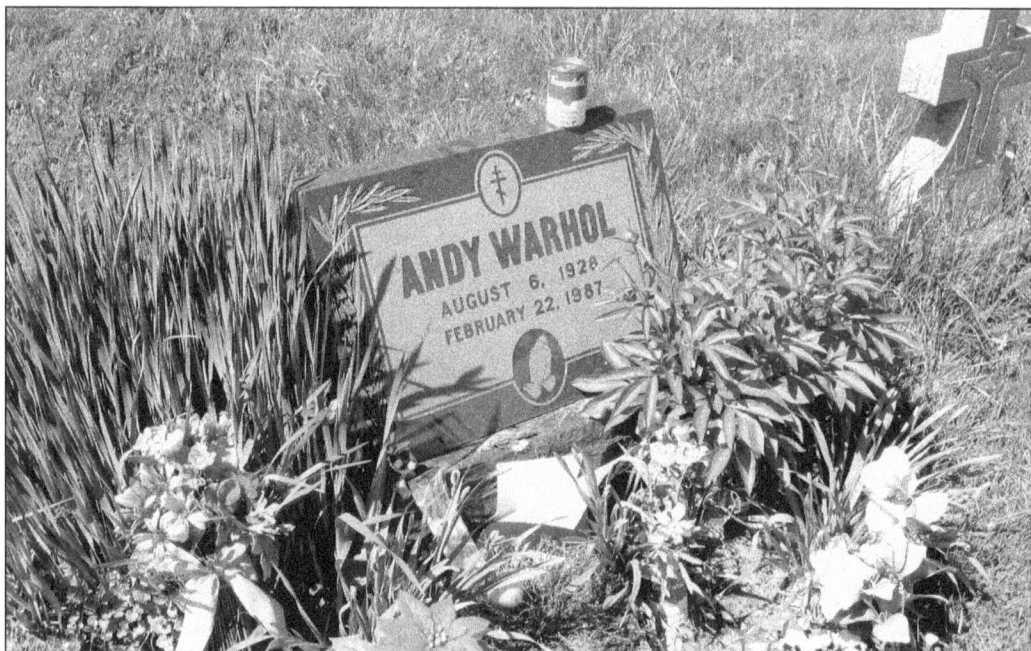

Famous pop artist Andy Warhol grew up in the South Hills of Pittsburgh. After his death in 1987, he was buried near his mother and father in Bethel's St. John the Baptist Cemetery on the hill above Washington Junction. (Courtesy of Richard and Patricia Kraft.)

Ruth Frisch and her children, from left to right, Bill, Skip, and Patricia, sit outside their Bethel Park home (right). Patricia Frisch Kraft and her husband, Richard, (below) have been longtime residents of Bethel Park. Dick and Pat run the Historical Room at Bethel Presbyterian Church and are actively involved in many of the historical aspects of Bethel Park. (Both, courtesy of Richard and Patricia Kraft.)

Rick Sebak, WQED producer of local and national documentaries, is one of the most beloved Bethel Park celebrities. Born and raised in Bethel, he went on to write, produce, and narrate his stylized American documentaries, such as *The Mon, the Al and the O, Kennywood Memories*, and *Things That Aren't There Anymore*. His recognizable voice and local nostalgic look at Pittsburgh's past made him a hometown icon. Above, he is already in his element in front of the television. (Both, courtesy of Rick Sebak.)

Rick Sebak
Producer/Writer/Narrator
All-American Documentaries
WQED Pittsburgh
www.wqed.org

Seven

HONOR AND SERVICE

Bethel Park has been fortunate to have local men and women who serve and protect the area from fire, personal harm, and the threat of war. The community gives thanks to the hardworking men and women who put their lives at risk every day as soldiers, police officers, and firefighters. Shown here, from left to right, are officers G. W. Kercher, O. P. Platz, J. V. Miskunas, W. J. Dabney, and W. Braum. (Courtesy of the Bethel Park Police Department.)

Over 80 years ago, the first volunteer fire company was established in Bethel in 1927. The fire department expanded with the growth of the township and ultimately built two more stations on Clifton Road and Milford Drive in the 1970s. (Both, courtesy of the Virgili family collection.)

The photograph above shows the volunteer firefighters outside the second station on Brightwood Road. A. M. Tischler was one of the original organizers of the department. Their first truck was a Model T (below). (Both, courtesy of the Bethel Park Fire Company.)

Parades are not complete without fire departments in line. These photographs are from parades during Bethel's 25th (left) and 26th (right) years of service. (Both, courtesy of the Bethel Park Fire Company.)

The company's fleet of trucks is shown here in 1967 at the Brightwood station next to Bethel Bakery. (Courtesy of the Bethel Park Fire Company.)

Bethel residents line Library Road, across from Henney's Funeral Home, to witness the fire company's burning drill. (Courtesy of the Virgili family collection.)

Above, the department starts orchestrating a drill as they climb to the second story of the house. Below, fire chief Reno Virgili (center) stands outside the house and confers with firefighters as they get ready for the drill. (Both, courtesy of the Virgili family collection.)

Chief Reno Virgili stands on the site where the Clifton station was being built in the 1970s. (Courtesy of Reno Virgili.)

The Bethel Park Volunteer Fire Company always ends the Memorial Day parade with Bethel Park pride and loud sirens, as seen in the procession below from the 1978 parade. (Courtesy of the Virgili family collection.)

The Bethel Park Police Department was established on April 1, 1941, when John Miskunas was appointed its first officer. By May, Miskunas was made chief of police, and he held this title until his death in February 1967. (Both, courtesy of the Bethel Park Police Department.)

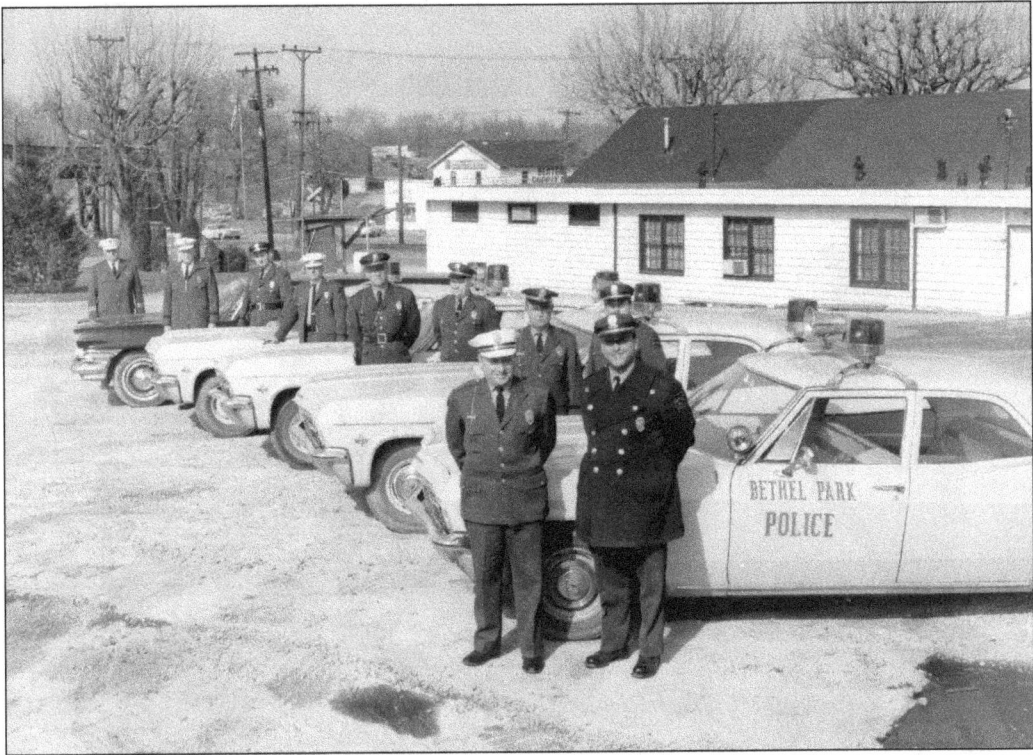

The Bethel Park officers stand outside their cars at the old municipal building on West Library Road above. Municipal council and department officers also gather for the formal photograph below. (Both, courtesy of the Bethel Park Police Department.)

The K-9 officers of Bethel Park have played an important role in the development of the department. Bethel Park has had 12 K-9 officers since its inception in 1960. From 1981 to 1989, Clarence "Skip" Hornak and Cong, pictured together here, were K-9 partners. Officer Frank Marks and Lord are Bethel's K-9 unit today. (Courtesy of the Bethel Park Police Department.)

The 1950 police department stands outside the new municipal building built above the old building on West Library Avenue. The 1970s department poses below for a formal picture with Mayor Peter Page. (Both, courtesy of the Bethel Park Police Department.)

JOSEPH
CHMELYNSKI
FATALLY WOUNDED
IN THE LINE OF DUTY
MARCH 5, 1948

Bethel Park has had the unfortunate circumstance of two officers being killed in the line of duty. Officer Joseph Chmelynski (left) was fatally wounded on March 5, 1948, and detective Lynn Sutter (below) was fatally wounded on March 26, 1987. A memorial has been erected outside the police department in their honor. (Both, courtesy of the Bethel Park Police Department.)

LYNN
SUTTER
FATALLY WOUNDED
IN THE LINE OF DUTY
MARCH 26, 1987

Bethel Park honors the thousands of veterans from every American war back to the Revolution. Brothers Peter (right) and Frank (below) Edwards served in the air force during World War II before coming home to run Brookside Lumber. (Both, courtesy of the Edwards family collection.)

125

Bethel business owners Ray Belback (left) and Rudy Miller (below) both served in the navy during World War II. A grand Veterans' Memorial was recently dedicated in front of the municipal building to honor all the Bethel Park soldiers who have served in the armed forces throughout history. (Left, courtesy of the Ray Belback family collection; below, courtesy of Ronald Miller.)

One of the oldest traditions in Bethel Park is the annual Memorial Day parade and service held at Bethel Cemetery. In 1884, they called this Decoration Day, as seen on the program at left, and it has been honored each year since. The photograph below depicts the Memorial Day service at Bethel Cemetery in 2010. It is held in the same fashion as in 1884, with recognition, prayer, and addresses to the public. Shown speaking is Bethel Park mayor Clifford Morton. (Right, courtesy of the Bethel Presbyterian Church collection; below, author's collection.)

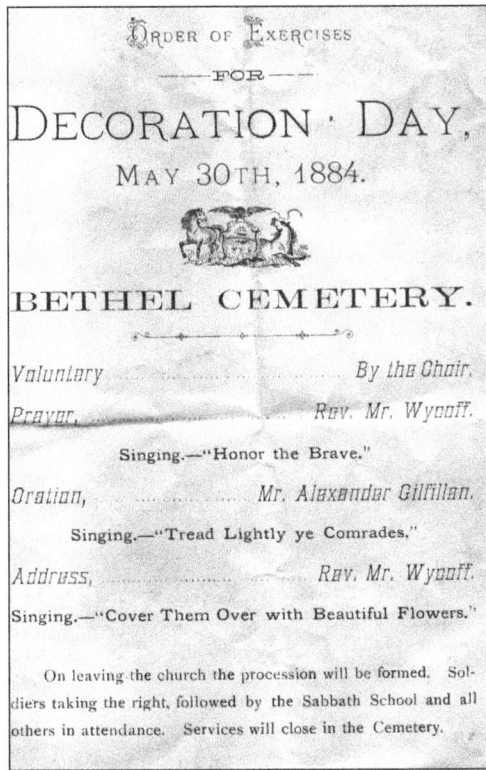

ORDER OF EXERCISES
----- FOR -----

DECORATION · DAY,
MAY 30TH, 1884.

BETHEL CEMETERY.

Voluntary	*By the Choir.*
Prayer,	*Rev. Mr. Wyooff.*

Singing.—"Honor the Brave."

Oration,	*Mr. Alexander Gilfillan.*

Singing.—"Tread Lightly ye Comrades."

Address,	*Rev. Mr. Wyooff.*

Singing.—"Cover Them Over with Beautiful Flowers."

On leaving the church the procession will be formed. Soldiers taking the right, followed by the Sabbath School and all others in attendance. Services will close in the Cemetery.

127

Visit us at
arcadiapublishing.com

www.ingramcontent.com/pod-product-compliance
Lightning Source LLC
Chambersburg PA
CBHW080559110426

42813CB00006B/1345